Laugh and Learn

Vocabulary

LAUGH AND LEARN VOCABULARY

THE #1 VOCABULARY TEACHER IS WORDPLAY HUMOR
INSIDE: JOKES, RIDDLES, CARTOONS, PUNS

STEPHAN DORLANDT

Laugh and Learn Vocabulary

Published by Gatekeeper Press
2167 Stringtown Rd, Suite 109
Columbus, OH 43123-2989
www.GatekeeperPress.com

StephanDorlandt@mail.com

Edited and Art Direction by Dasha Dorlandt

Illustrated by Joseph Rossow

ISBN (paperback): 9781662906725

To Maling Lu Walker, my beautiful wife, lover, friend and fellow sports fanatic. She was the catalyst for this book when she said, "why don't you write down all those jokes you keep making up, and put them in a book."

Special thanks are due to my lovely, talented daughter, Dasha Dorlandt, who made this book a reality by serving as both Art Director and Editor.

Finally, a shout out to all teachers everywhere who have a sense of humor.

Introduction

Laughing is fun; laughing is free; laughing is also quite serious you see.

Laughter as medicine. Ancient texts (e.g., *Proverbs* 17:22) and modern periodicals (e.g., *Reader's. Digest*) describe laughter as the best medicine. Medicinal benefits of a good chuckle include stress relief, improved circulation, increased endorphin release, and mental alertness. Then there is that side-effect to laughter: smiling.

Can laughter help us learn? According to the American Psychological Association:

> "Humor produces psychological and physiological benefits that help students learn."[1]

No wonder teachers with senses of humor are so effective, and fondly remembered.

Different jokes for different folks. That is, certain forms of humor are more educational than others. Slapstick humor, for example, doesn't lend itself to education. At the other end of the humor spectrum – replete with educational benefits – is wordplay.

Wordplay makes jokes out of words, their sounds and meanings. Wordplay is custom-made for the enjoyment of the language arts, and for vocabulary building.

---

1 American Psychological Association, Vol 37, No. 7, June 2006

Examples of wordplay include puns, riddles, sillynyms,[2] most of this book, and many advertising slogans.

How does wordplay build vocabulary? Two ways: psychologically, through motivation; and, physiologically, through brain exercise.

Motivation. It's a quid pro quo: figure out the wordplay joke – get the payoff (i.e., the laugh). It's the old carrot on a stick trick, with the punchline being the carrot. Therefore, when an unknown word presents itself in a wordplay joke, there is motivation to look up, or figure out, its meaning.

Brain exercise. One cannot be a successful athlete without physical exercise. Further, that exercise should target multiple muscle groups. By the same token, one cannot be successful at learning vocabulary without mental exercise, and the mental exercise should target multiple brain regions.

Wordplay gets the brain firing on all cylinders. According to the Association for Applied and Therapeutic Humor,[3] "getting the joke" activates the following regions/ purposes of the brain:

Right Hemisphere of the Cortex / intellectual analysis
Left Side of the Cortex / analyzes structure of joke
Frontal Lobe / social responses
Occipital Lobe / visual signals

---

[2] Sillynym means a silly and/or funny synonym. The author had the word, sillynym, added to the *Urban Dictionary*, 2018

[3] Website: aath.org

Motor sections / physical response to joke
Broca's Area / language control

Wordplay gives the brain a good workout because wordplay is intellectually demanding. Regarding puns for example,

> "The brain goes through some incredible gymnastics to capture the meaning of puns and if you think about it, it's incredibly complex. Especially when two words can sound exactly alike."[4]

What are the mental gymnastics of wordplay? They include language comprehension, cultural reference awareness, and pure thinking agility. These skills and abilities must be used in conjunction with each other; otherwise, the punchline may not be understood. For example, someone with a college level reading comprehension score may fail to understand a joke – if he or she lacks life experience and/or the capacity to think outside the box.

What is the level of difficulty of the wordplay in this book? The jokes in this book range from simple to sophisticated. They are in random order.

Welcome to a playground of words. Have fun, and don't be surprised if – along the way – your vocabulary grows. And that's no laughing matter.

---

[4] NPR WEEKEND EDITION, 5/11/2011, John Pollack quoted regarding his book, *The Pun Also Rises.*

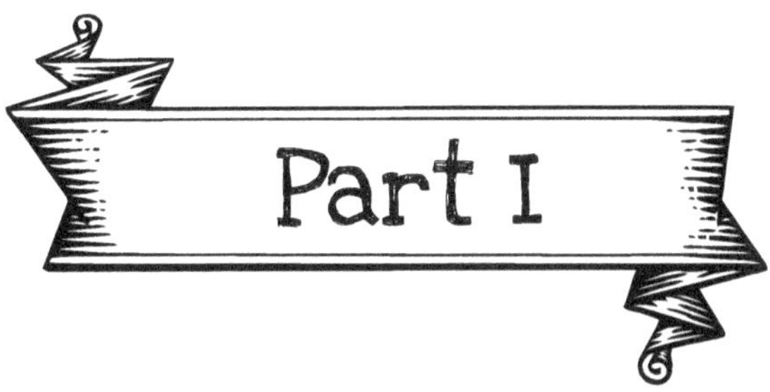
Part I

She wanted to use
the car pool lane.

How do you clean empty space?

With a vacuum cleaner

What kind of lumber is used to make movie sets?

Hollywood

What do you call food for a dog of Chinese origin?

Chow Chow chow

What do you call an undercover cop who has gone bad?

Vice versa

What do you call it when 007 ties you up?

BONDage

Where are the restrooms located on a boat?

On the poop deck

What do you call ones' last job?

The graveyard shift

What fruit prevents couples from running away to get married?

CAN'T ELOPE (cantaloupe)

What do you call a penthouse in Australia?

A down over

Where do lactose intolerant astronauts refuse to go?

The Milky Way

What do bullfighters order at Starbucks?

Café OLÉ (café au lait)

To which direction does bread rise?

To the yeast

What personal property cannot be covered by insurance?

The family jewels

How tall is the tv weather girl?

She is FAIR IN HEIGHT (Fahrenheit).

How do you cover your private parts with two vowels?

By using a diphTHONG.

What law or statute applies to hands?

The rule of thumb

What do you call a sunburn from hell?

SaTAN

What do you call a timepiece that doesn't work?

A stop-watch

What do you call post-surgical Kleenex?

Scar tissue

What do you call a deal you make with a horse to come to a halt?

Quid WHOA quo (pro)

What famous movie monster moonlights as an accountant?

Count Dracula

What is the hypnotic part of a building?

Its enTRANCE

What do you call practicing the funeral rites?

ReHEARSE

Why did the girl bring rouge to school?

Because she had to take a makeup test.

What do you call it when a woman tries, but fails, to get married?

Trying, but to no aVEIL (avail).

Why did the tracker take off his coat when he was getting closer to finding the missing person?

Because the trail was getting warmer.

What is the worst-smelling stage of life?

PEWberty (puberty)

What do you call a man known for clear, convincing arguments?

A CoGENT

Why did the insurance agent always take clients to an Indian restaurant?

To curry favor

What's a sillynym for a bullying attitude?

DeMEANor

With what emotion does a waiter view customers who leave no gratuity?

With anTIPathy

What mountain is equivalent to Mt. Everest?

TantaMOUNT

What do you call incisive, emphatic chanting?

TrenCHANT

What's a sillynym for brother?

AntitheSIS

Why did the sweaty girl take a pencil and paper to the restroom?

Because she wanted to draw a bath.

What large mammal knows how to communicate with cows?

The MOOSe

Why did the entrepreneur take the contract to SeaWorld?

He wanted to seal the deal.

What kitchen item did the author use to clean up the dirty language in his book?

An exSPONGE (expunge)

What do you call a Cherokee Indian's verbal invective against a Sioux Indian?

A diatribe

Why did the new student go to the bakery?

To enROLL

How do quarterbacks die?

They pass away.

What do you call an association of inept gardeners?

The bush league

What do you call a religious person pretending to be an atheist?

ProFEIGN (profane)

What is the saddest make of car?

A CRYSler (Chrysler)

What country has the highest number of bladder infections?

Urination

What do you call it when an oncologist says you have a terminal disease?

DIEagnosis (diagnosis)

What's the best aircraft for spying?

A LEERjet (Learjet)

What do you call addition in July?

SUMmer (Summer)

What is the most scientific fruit candy?

The fig Newton

What is a Tibetan ox's favorite drink?

ConYAK (cognac)

What can light the fire of a romantic relationship?

A matchmaker

What is the sunniest part of the body?

The solar plexus

What do you call a beautiful girl in the ICU?

An aCUTE patient

What do you call it when a queen uses the bathroom?

A royal flush

What kind of clothes should you bring to a haunted house?

Bewear (beware)

What do you call an angry psychiatrist?

TheraPISSED (therapist)

What type of spa takes lots of nerve to enter?

A chutSPA (chutzpah)

What do you call grammar that is married?

Conjugated

Is the pirate going to visit the optometrist?

AYE (eye)

What do you call an email sent by a pig?

Spam

What do you call the time when you're supposed to pay a sorcerer's bill?

VooDUE (voodoo)

What do you call a friend you sample wine with?

Your taste bud

Why did the cop carry a hammer in his holster?

He wanted to nail a bank robber.

Why did the lady in the Versace dress carry a derringer in her purse?

Because she was dressed to kill.

What do you call the mythology of single men?

BacheLORE (bachelor)

Why did the sailor want to go to Nashville?

He heard it was in the middle of TenneSSEA (Tennessee)

What do you call a nutritionist's feedback on what you had for dinner?

EvaluATE

Why did they call the greedy banker "Winchell's?"

Because he was a doughnut.

Why did the lonely guy go to the naval yard?

He was looking for a relationSHIP.

Why did the real estate agent demand that all her food be organic?

Because she heard it has excellent properties.

What word describes a bird flying in pain?

SORE (soar)

What does an unexpected winner in "The Bachelor" television show receive?

A SIRprize (surprise)

What song did Toto want to sing in The Wizard of Oz?

"Somewhere Rover the Rainbow"

Which state has the highest percentage of men?

The proSTATE

Why did the winner of the cow-milking contest get into the hall of fame?

Because he was legenDAIRY (legendary)

Which geometric shape attempts to complete a task?

TRYangle (triangle)

What do you call a cancer doctor who is available 24 hours a day?

An ONCALLogist (oncologist)

What do you call garish divinity?

GODiness (gaudiness)

What do you call an ugly death in ancient China?

DIE NASTY (dynasty)

What do you call a large goat's jewelry?

RAMbling

Where should one ship a woman's evening gown?

To the adDRESS

How do you say goodbye to early morning moisture?

ADEW (adieu)

What do you call having your picture taken at your fattest angle?

AdiPOSE (adipose)

What do you call foolish behavior at the stern of a ship?

DAFT

What do you call pain and discomfort stemming from drinking too much beer?

ALEment (ailment)

What do you call telling the police you were shopping at the mall at the time of the crime?

AliBUY (alibi)

What do you call hope for pain?

AngWISH (anguish)

What do you call nullifying something by being tardy?

AnnihiLATE

What do you call the recognition of value in a woman?

AppreSHEation (appreciation)

Which vegetable can stop your breathing?

ArtiCHOKE

What do you call having too much firewood in storage?

BackLOG

What do you call a psychiatrist singing hip hop?

Shrink-RAP (wrap)

What word describes pain in the patella?

AgoKNEE (agony)

What do you call a spouse with a gambling problem?

The BETter half

Where should an alcoholic's casket be placed?

On a BEER (bier)

What verb tense is overlooked in grammar?

InadverTENSE (inadvertence)

What do you call a biographer's bill?

BiograFEE (biography)

What do you call a hawk that kneels at church?

A bird of PRAY (prey)

What do you call a king
who likes to measure things?

A ruler

What do you call a pig
that puts you to sleep?

A boar (bore)

What do you call a medieval
town for gophers?

A BOROUGH (burrow)

What kind of hot dog do juvenile delinquents eat?

BRATwurst

What's do you call a hiding place for currency?

A cash cache

What do you call it when a sheep is in distress?

CaLAMBity (calamity)

What is a flowery word for an automobile-obsessed country?

CARnation

What do you call a cat taking a shot of tequila?

Catnip

Part 2

Where do ghosts surf?
MaliBOO (Malibu)

What gravity-like force makes people save money?

CentriFRUGAL (centrifugal)

Why did the techie take his computer to the shoe store?

To reboot it.

What do you call a large cat that doesn't play fair?

A CHEATa (cheetah)

What do you call it when the temperature and humidity get married?

CliMATE

What do you call an adult beverage for roosters?

COCKtail

What fish works as an administrator at a university?

A sarDEAN (sardine)

What do you call an amphitheater where you see your boyfriend?

ColoSEEHIM (colosseum)

What do you call a pugnacious, nocturnal mammal?

ComBAT

What did the photographer say to the fidgety model?

"ComPOSE yourself"

What do you call meditating over a piece of china?

ContemPLATE

What do you call clothes you can't take off?

UnBAREable (unbearable)

What do you a Carfax for an American sports car?

CorVETte (vet)

Why did the guy wear flannel pajamas on his first date?

He wanted the girl to cotton to him.

What do you call a borrowed tropical storm?

A cycLOAN (cyclone)

Why did the lumberjack take out a handsaw on the boat?

He was told to debark.

What do you call an inhabitant of a Buddhist temple?

A deniZEN

What do you call it when twins cry?

DeSPAIR

What is a cannibal's favorite magazine?

Reader's Digest

What do United Nations' ambassadors wipe their shoes on?

The diploMAT

What do you call a map to a priest's residence?

DiRECTORY

What do undertakers call a humid day?

EmBALMy

What is the best part of a fish to eat for pain relief?

The endorFIN (endorphin)

What do you call a supernatural experience in a dentist's office?

TranscenDENTAL

What letter is evil?

The evil i (eye)

What do you call the restoration of a painting depicting the Passion of Christ?

CruciFIX

What do you call an adolescent from Florence?

FlorenTEEN (Florentine)

What do you call a formal, agonizing dinner dance?

A foul ball

What is a horse's favorite wine?

ChardoNEIGH (Chardonnay)

What is a place you can arrive at before you get there?

A halfway house

What do you call getting a $1,000.00 bonus for hitting a home run?

A grand slam

According to medieval legend,
what is the most sacred ale?

The Holy GrALE (grail)

Why did the gardener take a shrub to Las Vegas?

He wanted to hedge a bet.

What do you call a Homo Sapien
who cuts down trees?

A HEW MAN (human)

What is a bully of an allergen?

HistaMEAN (histamine)

Why did the gardener bring
his equipment to the dance?

Because it was a HOEdown.

How do you hang a triangle?

On its hypoteNUSE (noose)

What country exists only in the mind?

ImagiNATION

What do call eating something funny?

InJEST (ingest)

What do you call shredding two different types of cheese at the same time?

InteGRATE

What do you call a dancing roach?

A jitterbug

What do you call the avoidance of family members?

KinDRED

What is the worst kind of siesta?

A kidNAP

What amount of medicine is given for praise?

KuDOSE (kudos)

What's an IT term for putting an entire hamburger in your mouth?

A megaBITE (byte)

What do you use to meet someone?

A meter

What resulted when the guy got lost in the fog on the way to the airport?

He MIST his flight (missed).

What can you say about a produce manager who successfully rearranges the vegetables?

He or she doesn't miss a BEET (beat).

On what type of bars do you hang upside down?

Monkey bars

Why did the fellow dress up like Othello when he went to the buffet?

Because he wanted MOOR (more).

Why did the busy man refuse to eat lunch?

Because he already had too much on his plate.

Why did the man take
a cow to the bank?
He wanted to beef
up his assets.
FINANCES

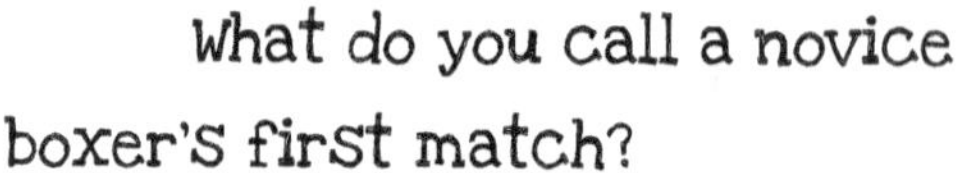

What do you call a novice boxer's first match?

A neoFIGHT (neophyte)

What do you call a senior woman's rear end?

An old wive's TAIL (tale)

What do you call signing up for a breadmaking class?

EnROLLment

What do you call a large number of impoverished people leaving a place?

OutPOORing (outpouring)

What kind of trousers do aquatic birds wear?

PantaLOONS

What do you call a minister who guides you around a church?

A paSTOUR (pastor)

What does a poncho cover?

A paunch

What do you call waves of proteins?

PepTIDES

What do you call a rice dish that tickles?

PiLAUGH (pilaf)

What was Eve's favorite fruit?

Adam's apple

What does a fired, female employee wear under her dress?

A pink slip

Why did the young man steal the frying pan?

He wanted a POACHED egg.

What do you call a basketball player from a small town?

PoDUNK

What is an anti-inflammatory zone?

CortiZONE (cortisone)

What barrio do priests live in?

In the priesthood

What do you call an enticing Chinese vase?

CharMING

What does an estate lawyer use to go fishing?

ProBAIT (probate)

What do you call the wherewithal to pay all debts?

ABILLity (ability)

What word describes two vegetables?

ProDEUCE (produce)

What do you call an unimaginative mosaic?

Prosaic

What do you call religious grammar?

Proverb

What do you call having a lollipop in a group setting?

PubLICK (public)

What do you call a boat on which sad people are free to cry?

A WAILing ship (whaling)

What flying animal works at the circus?

An acroBAT

What is a physics term for a large stomach?

QuanTUM

Why did the tourists die at the Natural History Museum?

Because they went to the DIEarama (diorama).

What do you call a tennis player in the mafia?

Racketeer

What do you call inflicting damage via the olfactory sense?

REEKING damage (WREAKING)

What is the deadliest type of storm?

A RAIN of terror (reign)

What do you call a line of people waiting to be airlifted?

ReSQUEUE (rescue)

What is a regretful sandwich?

A RUEben

What do lion's call a really good time?

Rip-roaring

What sport is played on carpet?

RUGby

What is the most valuable urine?

RuPEE (rupee)

What snack is larcenous?

A safecracker

Why did grandpa refuse to say a prayer at dinner?

He was saving grace.

How do con artists run?

They SCAMper.

What do you call it when a grizzly carries a rifle?

BEARing arms

What do you call a seven seas' tour?

SightSEAing (sightseeing)

What do you call it when a father runs away from his family?

SkeDADdle

What do you call a street with slippery driveways?

Skid row

What do you call an old form of idiomatic speech that is missed?

Auld SLANG Syne (lang)

What measures the equpment at a playground?

A slide rule

What's another name for the lumber business?

IndusTREE (industry)

What's a sillynym for hearing aid?

Engineer (ENGINE EAR)

Part 3

What do you call a chicken with sunglasses?

EGGcentric (eccentric)

Why did the boy take shoe polish when he took his girlfriend out?

He took a shine to her

What do they call the winning ice cream in Vegas?

Sherbet (sure BET)

What do you call emptying out the contents of a handbag?

DisPURSE (disperse)

What do you call differentiating between wishes?

DistingWISH (distinguish)

Where do shoppers get beat up?

At the MAUL (mall)

What is something frightening on the face?

MaSCAREa (mascara)

What do you call a lousy hip-hop concert?

A bum rap

What did the pyromaniac want from his boss?

A RAIZE (raise)

What fish always changes the subject?

Red herring

What do you call an inadequate business plan for a bakery?

Half-baked

What do you call a manual of fingers?

A handbook

What did the girl wear at the equestrian center?

A halter top

What writing instrument is used
to describe hereditary traits?

Genetic marker

What is the deadliest
side to be on?

GenoSIDE (genocide)

What word describes
down-to-earth, clear reasoning?

GeoLOGIC

What do you call the negative effects of excess belly fat?

Hazardous WAIST (waste)

What do you call aquatic birds that are easy to fool?

GULLible

What word describes a motivated gardener?

GungHOE (ho)

What does a professional teaser have?

ExperTEASE (expertise)

Why did the quarreling couple go to the dry cleaners?

To iron out their differences.

Why did the family put the bill collector in the horse's stable?

To stall him

What do you call the point when a marriage becomes boring and tedious?

Stalemate

What do you call a plan to acquire jewelry?

A strataGEM

What do you call the prohibition of drinking alcoholic beverages for attorneys?

Disbar

How did the minister get injured?

He fell from grace.

What is a joint that kids love to visit?

DiSKNEEland (DiSneyland)

What is a game that makes things evident?

Display

Where can one find a meteorological drawer?

Inside the weather bureau

What is a mental illness that doesn't cost you anything?

SchizoFREEnia (Schizophrenia)

What word describes giving a group of people something beautiful?

DistriBEAUT (Distribute)

Why did the arbitrator place the corporation's bylaws in boiling water?

He wanted to dissolve the corporation.

What do you call two unrelated lines of poetry?

Diverse

What do you call a cut-up corpse?

DiviDEAD (Divided)

What grows on a heavenly trellis?

Divine

What do you call it when someone has two big toes on the same foot?

Ditto

Why did the student hold her nose as she opened a textbook?

She was about to dive into her studies.

What kind of smell does a museum tour guide have?

Docent (SCENT)

What do you call a television show about a hospital?

A docudrama

What do you call a crooked politician running for office again?

An incumBENT

What country is the opposite of fictitious?

ISREAL (Israel)

What do you call giving an opinion about a tree?

Opine

What animal do you find at funerals?

PallBEARer

What do you call a tournament among birds?

A round-robin

What do you call a quick
glance at the top of Mt. Everest?

A PEAK (peek)

What do you call a small,
unimportant cat?

A MEERkat (a mere cat)

What word describes a karate blow to metaphysics?

PSyKICK (pSychic)

Why did the patient duck her appointment with the doctor?

Because she heard he was a quack.

What part of a song calls for an umbrella?

The refrain (RAIN)

What is the most regretful pie?

RUEbarb (rhubarb)

What do pirates call dogs they don't like?

ScalaWAGS

Where did the chain break at the zoo?

At the weakest lynx (LINK)

What do you call trying to separate fact from fiction?

AnaLIESzing (analyzing)

What do you call an armadillo's minor offense?

A peccadillo

What is the most egotistical garment?

A stuffed shirt

What do you call a bee with no balance?

A stumble bee

What do you call the class of animals with vision?

SpeSEES (species)

Why did the proper gentleman have to pay more than other customers?

Because he had to pay a SIRcharge (surcharge)

What do you call an orchestra composed of bogus musicians?

A symPHONY

What do you call a man whose conversations always go off course?

TanGENT

What do you call a stock market named after an ancient Eastern religion? The Tao Jones

What do you call a pyromaniac's favorite ballad?

A torch song

What do you call a diaphanous dad?

Transparent

What is a musician's favorite piece of silverware?

A tuning fork

How many adolescents are there in the world?

UmpTEEN

How do you describe something that might be big?

AmBIGuous

What do you call washing your horse tack?

A bridal shower

Why did the hairdresser call for security?

Because her customer had unruly hair.

Where did the maître d' seat the ghost?

In a BOOth

What do you call a bouquet of flowers that cannot be put into a container?

EVASEive (evasive)

What kind of automobile do church bishops drive?

ViCAR (vicar)

What is a true dance?

The Virginia REAL (Reel)

After dismissing the case, how did the judge leave the courtroom?

He WAIVED goodbye (waved)

What do you call a Caucasian with a sting?

WASP

What's a sillynym for a fanny pack?

A WAIST basket (waste)

When do people have the least energy?

On WEAK days (week)

What do you call a strange deer?

WeirDOE (weirdo)

What do you call the arrest of someone in a business suit?

A white collar

What is the dumbest kind of knowledge?

WisDUMB (wisdom)

What do you call it when an art student leaves a portrait class?

Withdrawing

What is the biggest member of the butterfly family?

MamMOTH

Part 4

Why was the actress so hungry?
Because she only had a small ROLE (roll).

Why did the Soldier bring a diamond ring to the battlefield?

He wanted to engage the enemy.

What do you call the genetic love of baking?

InBREAD (inbred)

What letter has the most words?

A newsletter

What do you call someone who puts poison in Cheerios?

A CEREAL killer (serial)

Where did our ancestors swim?

In the gene pool

What did the narcissistic politician use to get his message out?

The MEdia

What field of physics relates to archery?

ARROWynamics (aerodynamics)

What branch of science deals with sighs?

SIGHchology (psychology)

What do you call it when a waiter serves you a porterhouse instead of filet mignon?

A misSTEAK (mistake)

Why did the weightlifter go to the morgue?

He wanted to do dead lifts.

Which punctuation mark goes to the winner?

The apoSTROPHY (apostrophe)

What do you call the family tree of Levi Strauss?

JEANeology (genealogy)

What's a sillynym for a horse story?

A ponyTALE (ponytail)

Why did the astronaut take off his underwear when his space capsule re-entered the earth's atmosphere?

Because he knew he was going to be de-briefed.

What do you call a flammable brassiere?

ComBUSTible

What do you call someone who dislikes cheese?

Persona non grata

What dog breed cries?

ChiWAHWAH (chihuahua)

What do you call an honest discussion at Thanksgiving?

Talking turkey

How did the artist get the obnoxious man out of her studio?

She brushed him off.

What do you call a plethora of pet stores under one roof?

AniMALL (animal)

Why was the stonemason shocked when he was laid off?

Because he had taken his job for GRANITE (granted).

During what occasion did Einstein come up with the theory of relativity?

At a family reunion

What U.S. city is preferred by female horses?

FILLYdelphia (Philadelphia)

What do you call it when someone pirouettes and vocalizes simultaneously?

DanSING (dancing)

What is the favorite state among carpenters?

ArkanSAW

Why did the car need a vacation?

It was tired.

What do you call a foreboding astrological forecast?

A HORRORScope (horoscope)

What dish is never served at dinner parties?

Petri dish

What do you call the charge the customer receives at a café?

CofFEE

What's a cannibal's favorite mammal?

The AUNTeater (anteater)

What is Superman's favorite sandwich?

A hero

Why did the conman go to the insurance company?

Because of his LIEability (liability)

How do you label a housekeeper in Beijing?

Maid in China

What Olympic sport is performed by beauticians?

Curling

What do you call televised, post-operative exercise?

Dancing with the scars

What kind of roll can feel a dozen people?

A casseROLL (casserole)

What do you call a boat that is never soft?

A hardship

Why did the man take a blanket
to his insurance agent?

Because he wanted full coverage

What do you call a female horse at night?

A nightmare

Where is the most boring place in Alabama?

It's over YAWNder (yonder).

What is the most religious church in Hollywood?

Shirley Temple

Why was John Smith scared?

Because he was dating PocaHAUNTus (Pocahontas).

Where do fibbers hang out?

At the LIEbrary (library)

What do you call the history of the Ford Motor Company?

An AUTObiography

What do you call fear of Vietnamese cuisine?

PHObia

Where do writing instruments go when they're bad?

To the PENitentiary

What do you call looking for a nudist beach?

A strip search

Why did the lady accountant get arrested for indecent exposure?

Because of her bottom line.

What flowers kiss?

TWOLIPS (tulips)

Why did the rabbit go to the beauty salon?

For a hare cut.

What is an accountant's favorite piece of bedding?

A spreadsheet

Why didn't the priest smile?

He was feeling cross.

On what legal grounds was the duck arrested?

On suspicion of FOWL play (foul).

Why did the baseball batter wear decorative flags?

Because he was bunting.

What do you call the police file on a hip-hop singer?

A RAP sheet

Why are croissants wishy washy?

Because they're flaky.

What do you call a movie about physicians and surgeons?

A DOCumentary

Why is the river rich?

Because it has a bank.

What is the best morning meal for angina patients?

A hearty breakfast.

What do you call the business deal when a dancer gets re-hired at a strip club?

A reNUDE contract (renewed).

What do you call a canyon of bitter humor?

SarCHASM (sarcasm)

What do you call getting ready for a stroll?

PreAMBLE

What do you call a lobster's scab?

A CRUSTacean

Why was the IRS supervisor so tired?

Because his job was taxing.

What does an IT person call the area between two breast enhancements?

Silicon valley

Where does the president go when he wants to fly?

The West Wing.

What do tired eyes and a campground have in common?

Sleeping bags

Why are airport runways like football?

They have touchdowns.

What do you call a preachy German Shepherd?

DOGmatic

Why did the fish go to jail?

Becausae it was GILLty (guilty).

What is the saddest tea?

PiTEA (pity)

What does a cat see when it looks through binoculars?

A PURRview (purview)

Why did the golfer bring his computer to the golf course?

Because he wanted to hit a hard drive.

What do you call a metropolitan area with lots of liars?

MendaCITY

What is the craziest mode of transportation?

A LOCOmotive

What part of the body never says yes?

The nose

Why did they call the baseball pitcher a Soprano?

Because of his high pitch.

How did the drill put the carpenter to sleep?

Because it was boring.

What do you call a cheap hotel for dogs?

A fleabag

Where does the Devil go for transportation?

To the HELLiport (heliport)

What do you call a mixed group of ballistic rockets?

MISSLEaneous (miscellaneous)

What is the most infamous bird?

Owl Capone

What do you call a mallard that leads musicians?

conDUCKtor (conductor)

What inclement weather is good for problem solving?

BrainSTORMING

What is the name of a shattered art style?

Baroque (broke)

How does one enter the United Nations?

Through the ambassaDOOR (ambassador)

What's another name for rent-a-cop?

PoLEASE (police)

What do you call a vampire's comments on the radio?

A sound bite

What do frogs and toads lie so much?

Because they are amFIBians (amphibians).

What branch of mathematics comes in handy when doing inventory in a lingerie department?

AlgeBRA

What is the smallest pig?

A HAMster

What do you call a tuna fish with a six pack?

AlbaCORE

What kind of pet is impossible to adopt at an animal rescue?

Pet peeve

What do you call a mistake made by an oral surgeon?

AcciDENTAL

Why did the cop take the crook to the library?

To book him

What do Pacific Island women wear when they aren't right?

A saWRONG (sarong)

What kind of luggage does one use to carry underwear?

A briefcase

How do you bid someone adieux in Louisiana?

BYE YOU (bayou)

What condiment do you put on a Mexican hot dog?

Cinco de MAYO

Why did the basketball player take a paper and pencil to the game?

He wanted to draw a foul.

What do you call a wasp you don't have to pay for?

FreeBEE (freebie)

What's a Sillynym for Psychotic Boulevard?

Sociopath

What do you call a NSFW apple?

Hardcore

What museum serves the best Italian food?

The SpaGETTY (Spaghetti)

How does one factor a beet
into a carrot?

Use the Square root

What do you call a hug in baseball?

A Squeeze play

Part 5

Why did the dirty football player from New York cross the Hudson?
He wanted a NEW JERSEY.

What is a biting way to say "no"?

Gnaw

What is the most important part of the priest's arm during communion?

The EuchaWRIST (Eucharist)

Why did the model pray during the Vogue photo shoot?

Because she wanted to grace the cover.

Why is the geography of the brain so popular among ecologists?

It's environMENTAL.

What do you call a rabbit with a nice butt?

BUNny

What geometric shape gets rid of curses?

HEXaGONE (hexagon)

What do you call guessing someone's measurements?

HypotheSIZE

What did the guy say when he saw the offspring between a dog and a cat?

"What's dat?"

What kind of material did the Protestant use for her kitchen floor?

GenTILE

Why did the newscaster have a repairman on standby?

Because he was breaking news.

When is the best time to buy a boat?

When it's on SAIL (sale).

Why did the musician go to the store's linen department?

To buy sheet music

What is a royal, female accountant called?

A countess

What do you call speaking up for your husband or wife?

To eSPOUSE (espouse)

Why did the football fan dig a hole in the end zone?

He wanted to root for his team.

Where did the religious seamstress go to study dressmaking?

BethleHEM

Why was the duck called out in the softball game?

It FOWLED out (fouled)

Why did the salesclerk speak loudly when she asked, "Small, medium or large?"

Because she wanted to emphaSIZE.

What do you call hitting someone from India with a joke?

A PunJAB

What do you call a troupe of actors in a play about athletes?

A sportscast

What do you call an ice sculpture of a man with a six pack?

Abdominal Snowman (abominable)

What do you call getting ready for your appointment with a psychologist?

Preshrink

What do you call freedom and equal rights for advertising?

Ad-lib

What kind of arithmetic survives war?

AfterMATH

What do you call a monkey with an open mouth?

AgAPE

Why did God rest on the seventh day?

He wanted a SUNDAE (Sunday).

How does one say "kiss" in nerd terminology?

Interface

What do you call illegally chopping down a tree in a National Park?

TREESon (treason)

How does a French farmer push a wheel barrel to the barn?

A la carte

What do you call singing an aria in the bathtub?

A soap opera

What is the most sophisticated carnival?

Savoir FAIR (faire)

What do you call making a cup of tea quickly?

AlacriTEA (alacrity)

What do you call the method of chewing tough meat?

Al dente

What punctuation mark refers to someone who has had half the intestine removed?

Semicolon

Why did the fisherman bring putrid garbage to the riverbank?

Because he was fly-fishing.

What literary term describes bloody symbolism?

AlleGORY

What do you call gambling on vocabulary?

AlphaBET

What do you call an irascible flight attendant's disposition?

A bad altitude (attitude)

What is the most popular hair product in heaven?

AnGEL

Where does one put correspondence relating to England?

In the AngloFILE (anglophile)

What do you call pictures of lovemaking drawn by cartoonists?

AniMATED

When there is a fire in a department store, why do firefighters go first to the lingerie department?

Because that's where the hose is.

What's a word that describes preparing ground for planting?

AnteSEEDent (antecedent)

What branch of science says "I'm sorry?"

AnthrAPOLOGY (anthropology)

What do you call a girl who ruins a good time?

AntiFUNgal

What do you call the uppermost part of the chest muscle?

APECS (apex)

Why do lawyers hate lemons?

Because they're hard to apPEEL. (appeal)

What do you use to proclaim the revelation?

ApocaLIPS (apocalypse)

What nut has money?

The CASHew

What do you call it when a boy scout fails to tie a rope?

KNOT possible

What do you call a sick picture?

An ILLustration
(illustration)

What do you call a mafia boss in the last days?

ArmagedDON

How do you describe the way ones' mother smells?

AroMA

What do you call an archer with an attitude?

ARROWgant (arrogant)

What is a foolish name for 18 buttocks?

ASSiNINE (asinine)

What do you call electrocuting someone twice?

A revolt

What do you call nervous participation in social media?

Being atwitter (Twitter)

Why did the president give his State of the Union address in a cemetery?

Because it was a speech of grave importance.

What do you call a steer you can hear?

AudiBULL (audible)

What fruit takes care of children?

Au pair (pear)

Where do trucks sleep?

On a flatbed

What do you call a boat with pen and paper?

Authorship

Why did the dentist reject the award?

He didn't want the plaque.

What's the risk of driving a tipsy?

Autopsy

What do you call a newly constructed street?

AveNEW (avenue)

What do you call doing the cha-cha or salsa without touching, or looking at, your partner?

AvoiDANCE

Why did the sportscaster sprint around the field?

Because he was doing a running commentary.

What trigonometric function is used when a minor buys a car?

A COSIGN (cosine)

What do rodents like to play in Reno?

BaccaRAT

What sport is not good?

BADminton

What do you call consecutive face-to-face meetings?

Back-to-back

Where can you find the best Hollandaise?

In SAUCEalito (Sausalito)

What mode of transportation do political supporters use?

A bandwagon

What do you call musical coffee?

BanJOE (banjo)

What's an appropriate name for a tavern where everyone is admitted?

Bar none

What do you call a hair stylist who makes martinis?

BARber

What do you call a boat for worthy students?

A scholarSHIP

What do you call it when a loud dog boards a ship?

EmBARKing

Which baseball player makes the best pancakes?

The batter

What do seamstresses refuse to sew?

Belly buttons

What keeps Washington, D.C.'s pants up?

The beltway.

What form of media is preferred by weight lifters?

The bench press

What kind of platter is poison served on?

BeTRAY

How to movie theatres keep bugs out?

With the big screen

What do you call an insane trail?

PsychoPATH

What do you call a fence door with obscene language written on it?

A billingSGATE

What fraternal organization do male goats belong to?

Billy club

What do you call breaking news about a river?

Current events

What do you call legumes that have been in a fight?

Black-eyed peas

What game is played in the nude, but you can't see the other players?

Blindman's buff

What do you call a wormy coincidence?

A fluke

What do you call the hemorrhage of a barnlike structure?

Bloodshed

What is the edible part of the stock market?

Blue chips

What do you call an explosive bra?

A booby trap

Where do horses read?

In the bookstall

What kind of luggage does a despicable person use?

A scumBAG

What do you call an elastic musical group?

A rubber band

What piece of jewelry are you most likely to find on a loud horse?

A BRAYcelet (bracelet)

Which banking facility is found on a tree?

The branch office

What is a defiant form of Buddhism?

BraZEN

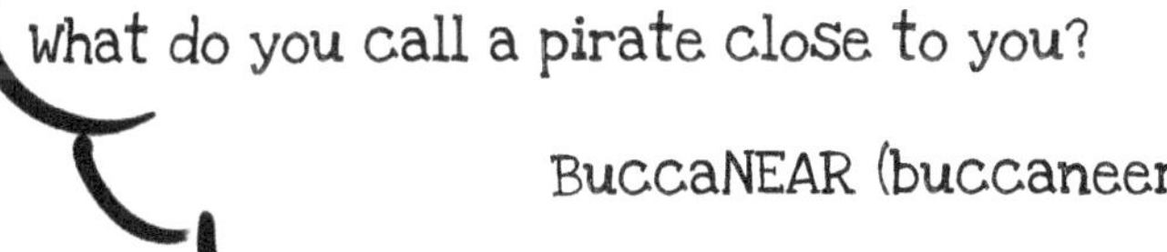

What do you call a pirate close to you?

BuccaNEAR (buccaneer)

Why did the housewife take pliers and a screwdriver into the kitchen?
She wanted to fix dinner.

What do you call a steer taking a siesta?

Bulldozer

Why did the golfer take her putter to the cemetery?

She wanted to bury a putt.

What do you call a pretty, isolated hill or mountain?

A BEAUT (butte)

Why did the advertising agent give his client a beehive?

To get some buzz.

What real estate deal will kill you?

Buying the farm.

What do you call the death of a country?

TermiNATION

How does a frank person describe a neutered dog?

By calling a spade a SPAYED (spade).

What do you call Christian soldiers on horseback?

Calvary

What is the most spiritual piece of lingerie?

CamiSOUL (camisole)

What do you call the time period beginning with the invention of photography?

CamERA

What hurts about being a politician?

The camPAIN (campaign)

What pasta gives hugs and kisses?

A caNOODLE

What do you call writing with upper case letters?

Capitalism

What do you call a repairperson getting prepared to go on a service call?

Prefix

When are Catholic leaders so good at mathematics?

When they use cardinal numbers.

What do you call a tight jean model's job?

A caREAR (career)

What do you call someone with intestinal gas who lives in a jungle?

CarmiNATIVE

Why did the vocalist bring a wheel barrel to the concert?

To make sure he could carry a tune.

What do you call an auction of merry-go-rounds?

A carouSELL (carousel)

What do surfers use to cook their meals?

A microwave

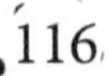

What is a purloined soap?

CaSTEAL (castile)

How does crime pay?

In law enforcement salaries

What instrument does a hair stylist use in a cave?

CataCOMB

What do you call a kitty that provokes a chemical reaction?

CATalyst

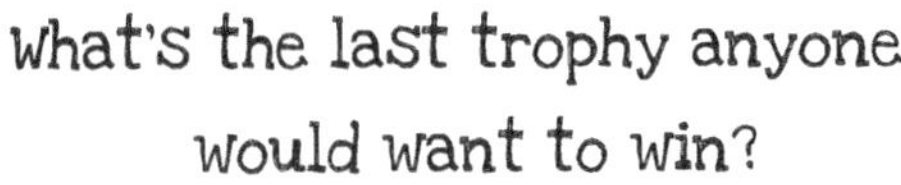

What's the last trophy anyone would want to win?

A catasTROPHY (catastrophe)

What do you call a negative smile?

A chaGRIN

What kind of candy can you write with?

CHAULKolet (chocolate)

What do you call the desire to change colors?

ChameleYEN (chameleon)

What is a sillynym for a spray-on tan?

CharlaTAN

What kind of stallion cramps your style?

Charley horse

How can you tell the rat was in a fight?

It has a mouse under one eye.

What do you call a bird that never picks up a check?

CHEEP (cheap)

Where do North African sheep go for conversation?

To the casBAA (casbah)

Why did Picasso's children have beautiful blood?

Because they inherited an artistic vein.

Why was the rooster cowardly?

It was chickenhearted.

What monkey is named after a flower?

The chimPANSY (chimpanzee)

What do you call Asian inspectors at an assembly plant?

Chinese checkers

What is the most religious member of the squirrel family?

The chipMONK (chipmunk)

Why did the wrestler's accountant get arrested?

Because he had a chokehold on his client's financials.

Where do electricians go to drink?

The cocktail circuit

What insect has ESP?

A clairvoyANT

What do you call a family of spies?

CLANdestine (clandestine)

What do you call poetry for the entire world?

UniVERSE

Why did the car buyer
take HandiWipes to the dealership?

She wanted a clean bill of sale.

Why did the runway model say "neigh?"

Because she was a clotheshorse.

What family hand-me-down jacket is unwearable?

The coat of arms

What is the easiest part of a highway for bicyclists to pedal?

On the COASTtline

Why did the football coach order KFC for his team?

He wanted to run the wishbone offense.

Why did the lady bring a basket to her meditation session?

She wanted to collect her thoughts.

Where do you deposit advertisements?

In a commercial bank

Part 6

Why did the guy drive a forklift to the bank?
BANK
He wanted to raise money.

What is the most condescending dog?

Great DEIGN (Dane).

What do you call a potter's salary?

URNings (earnings)

How is the hierarchy of woodpeckers established?

By the pecking order

Who are the best three people to interview if you want to know the general public's feeling about an issue?

Tom, Dick, and Harry

What do you call a business inside a small house?

A cottage industry

What do you call a designer gown that is labeled "Small" but is actually a large?

CounterFIT (counterfeit)

What is the most expensive bat?

A country club

Where does a county commissioner sit?

On the county seat

What's a sillynyn for the Love Boat?

Courtship

What do you call belief in the palatability of a certain food?

CrEDIBLE

What do you call burning a crucifix?

Crossfire

What do you call standing in line to play pool?

A cue

What do you call a random choice
of which shirt to wear?

Off the cuff

Why did the musician bring
scissors to the studio?

He wanted to cut an album.

What Buddhist takes too much time?

DALLY Lama (Dalai)

What do you call a sofa you can tie a boat to?

A davenPORT

What religious holiday is best for tuning your piano?

On the Day of Atonement

What is the worst kind of timepiece?

Deathwatch

Why did the angry blackjack dealer throw a pack of cards at the pit boss?

He wanted to deck him.

What do you call erasing a song you just wrote?

Decompose

Why did the psychiatrist take the temperature of his patients?

To see if there was a high degree of stress.

What's another name for tailwind?

DerriAIR (derrière)

Why did the impatient passenger kill himself at the airport?

He was dying to go.

Why did the judge practice subtraction?

To figure out the difference between right and wrong.

What's a word that describes an arduous sect?

DiffiCULT

What do you call someone who gets dinged on a boat?

DINGEE (dinghy)

Why does the mafia take their cash to a money launderer?

Because it's dirty money.

What do you call a premature parrot?

An early bird

Why did the apologetic man have a full stomach?

Because he had to eat his words.

What do you call an angel's sweatshirt?

Sainthood

What is the most desirable kind of static?

Ecstatic

What do you call residential accommodations for ten people?

A TENement

What do you call pretentious feet?

EfFEET (effete)

What do you call a Chinese omelet that's not old?

Egg foo YOUNG (yong)

Why did the chemistry professor dress in survival gear?

Because he was battling the elements.

What do you call the place
where you trade cows for pigs?

Stock exchange

How do you feel when you get
caught with your pants down?

EmBAREASSED (embarrassed)

What do you call a pride of loud, female lions?

A SoROARity (Sorority)

What U.S. mountain chain
could be called the Title Mountains?

The APPELATION Mountains (Appalachian)

What do you call
experiencing a divine moment
while looking at someone's backside?

EpiFANNY (epiphany)

What do you call an apparition of a male cat?

PhanTOM

What do you call the sense of balance received from a psychiatric medicine?

EquiLIBRIUM (equilibrium)

What do you call refusing to eat something?

eSCHEW

What did the male sheep say to the female sheep?

I love ewe (YOU)

What do you call pretending to faint?

Feint

Why did the Moroccan man wear a hat to the police station?

He wanted to fez up to the crime.

What is an example of an embezzled dairy product?

Skimmed milk

Who is the best musician in the ocean?

The fiddler crab

What is the best language to complete something with?

Finnish

What is something you can go to jail for fixing?

A boxing match

What is a skeleton's favorite sport?

Skulling

What geometric shape describes a parrot that flew away?

POLLY GONE (polygon)

What do you call suing an airline?

A flight suit

Where do lousy, old movies retire?

To a flophouse

Why was the chimney sweep always sick?

Because he always had the FLU (flue).

What do you call immobilizing a limb before its broken?

Forecast

Why was the genealogist confused?

She couldn't figure out how she had FOUR FATHERS (forefathers).

What do you call nausea caused by looking at bloody evidence in a crime lab?

ForenSICK (forensic)

What is the first step in building shelves for dictionaries?

The frame of reference

Why did the writer want to live in the skyscraper?

Because it had 70+ stories.

What do call it when a revolutionary is released from jail?

A free radical

What do you call a small rug given to a basketball player?

A free throw

Why did the patient refuse to pay the doctor bill?

He wanted to be pain free.

What's something you'll never see at a couture show in Paris?

French dressing

Why did the lender walk behind the borrower?

Because he fronted him the money.

What do you call a parsimonious girl?

FruGAL

Why did the senator bring candy to the debate?

Because he wanted to fudge the issue.

What is a deadly mix of blue and yellow?

GanGREEN (gangrene)

What do you call recent income?

ReveNEW (revenue)

What do you call it when a harmonica player complains incessantly?

Harping

What is the preferred religion among rabbits?

HARE Krishna

What do you call a coiffure for suicidal people?

HAIRY-kari (hari)

What kitchen utensil is used for
political contributions?

Funnel

What kind of bird makes the best street vendor?

A hawk

What do you use to hit
people with when they refuse to exercise?

A health club

What is the hottest
massage technique?

The heat stroke

What do you call evil hay?

Heinous

Where do people listen after they die?

In the HEARafter (hereafter)

What drinking vessel makes a sound?

A hicCUP

Why did the musician wear boxing gloves?

He wanted to hit the right note.

What do you call it when someone takes a pig to a pawnshop?

Ham hocks

What do you call a disease in your home?

Homeopathy

What do bees use to style their hair?

A honeycomb

What is the smartest bread in the bakery?

The honor roll

Which chemical messengers
emit sounds of pleasure?

HorMOANS (hormones)

What do you call an English
bathroom with boisterous people?

HulabaLOO

What do you call the long bone that makes us laugh?

The HUMORus (humerus)

What pronoun praises God?

HIM (hymn)

What's a sillynym for fender bender?

InciDENT

What do you call official permission to lie?

LIEcense (license)

What do you call something hidden but really cool?

IncogNEATO (incognito)

What do you call a steer too mean for the rodeo?

IncorrigiBULL (incorrigible)

What do you call a servant with false teeth?

Indentured

What does the sense of smell rely on?

InSTINK (instinct)

What do you call two stories that share the same theme and moral principle?

ComPARABLE

What's the sexiest thing you can do between math and history classes?

Intercourse

Part 7

What do you call a fortune teller with healing words?

What do you call a dinosaur with the flu?

JuraSSICK (Jurassic)

What do you call a young river?

JuveNILE

What do you call a Buddhist mother?

KarMA

What is the most remorseful mammal?

KangaRUE (kangaroo)

Why did the security guard carry a paring knife at night?

To keep his eyes peeled.

In which state do people never wear their shirttails out of their pants?

KenTUCKy

What do you call a stupid monarchy?

A kingDUMB (kingdom)

What word describes choking on a lollipop?

Lollygag

Why did the politician go to a veterinarian during his last days in office?

Because he was a lame duck.

What did the attorney wear to court?

A lawSUIT

What do you call an actress playing the role of tour guide?

The leading lady

What do you call a gymnastics' move made at great speed?

Lickety-split

What do you call lazy bread?

A loaf

What kind of reptile is found in night clubs?

Lounge lizard

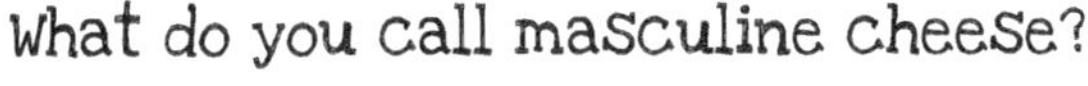

What do you call masculine cheese?

MaCHEESEmo (machismo)

What is the angriest street in New York City?

MADISon Avenue

What do you call a men's whirlpool?

A MALEStrom (maelstrom)

What net has no holes?

A magNET

How much does a chest X-ray weigh?

A mammogram

What was the policeman's status after he threw down his baton?

He was out of whack.

Where is the best place to buy a bonnet or beret?

ManHATtan

What is an unforgettable street?

Memory Lane

What type of cycle is impossible for men to ride?

Menstrual cycle

What do retail store managers gamble with?

MerchanDICE (merchandise)

Who is in charge of cleaning the ocean?

The mermaids

What is the drink no bartender will make?

A Molotov cocktail

What do you call the rear end of a rooster?

Cocktail

What do you call a fireplace with only one piece of firewood?

A monoLOG (monologue)

How could the duck tell that the goose was in love with the swan?

Because he kept taking a gander at it.

What do you call deadly unrest during Easter season?

VioLENT (violent)

Why do tabloid newspapers need gardeners?

To do the muckraking

What do you call a coffee cup
with a persons' face on it?

A mug

What kind of cereal inspires poets?

MUSEli (muesli)

What do they call quiet
mothers in England?

Mum

What is a dress that cows talk about?

Muu-muu

What do you call a woman who almost doesn't get married?

A near miss (MISS)

What do you call a sister who is your enemy?

NemeSIS

What do you call something stupid added to the end of a report?

AddenDUMB (addendum)

What do you call a hen's saving's account?

A nest egg

What is the bottom line for a fisherman's accountant?

The net profit

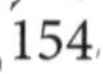

What word means always more?

Nevertheless

What do you call a Santa Claus
who refuses to give gifts?

St. Nix

What do you call a cactus with no friends?

NoPAL

Why did the young lady
take a stethoscope to the café?

She wanted to nurse a cup of coffee.

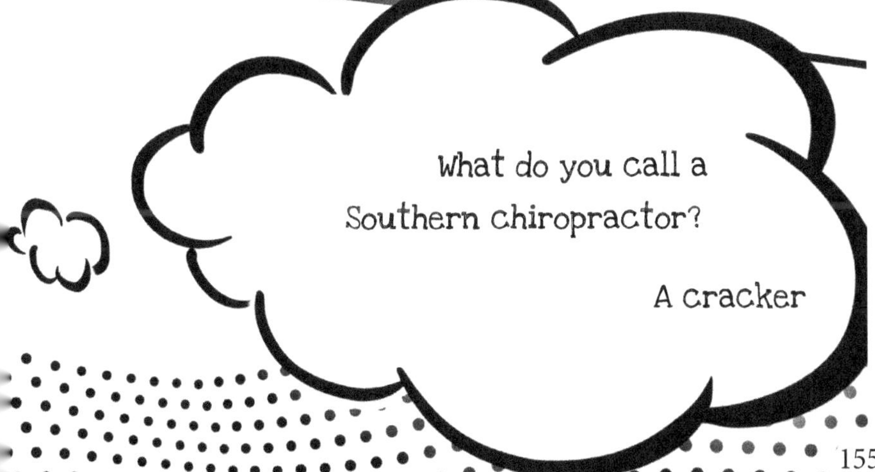

What do you call a
Southern chiropractor?

A cracker

What do you call magic tricks performed at birth?

ObsteTRICKS (obstetrics)

What do you call the teeth on the western side of your mouth?

OcciDENTAL

What do you call being exiled on account of your physical stature?

OstraSIZED (ostracized)

What women's garments are worn just outside of town?

The outskirts

What atmospheric layer are you in when surprised?

The OH zone (ozone)

What animal prays the most?

What type of scientist needs to get out in the sun?

PALEeontologist (paleontologist)

What word describes the violent destruction of a dress?

MayHEM

Why did the beggar go to northwest Florida?

To panhandle

Where does the Pope swim?

In the papaSEA (papacy)

What do you call a kitchen filled with pies?

OccuPIEd

What do you call a ten-cent example?

ParaDIME (paradigm)

What vegetable do you cut with small scissors?

ParSNIP

Why did the lazy employee give a dollar to hardworking colleague?

He wanted to pass the buck.

Where do ill condiments go for medical care?

Mayo Clinic

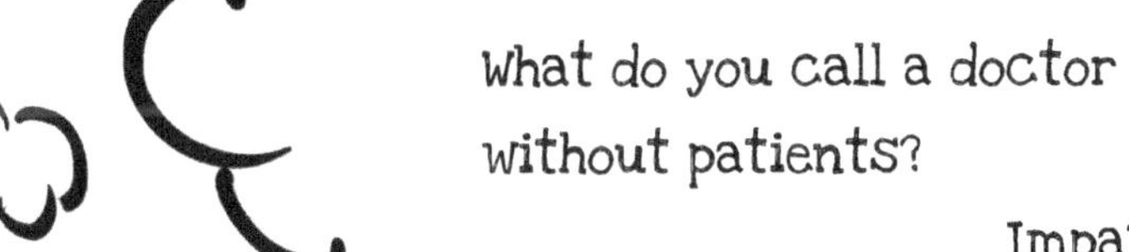

What do you call a doctor without patients?

Impatient

What legendary superhero needed a podiatrist?

Paul Bunyan (bunion)

Why did the lady take an inhaler when she went to the jewelry store?

Because she knew she would have to pay through the nose.

What do you call a Chinese leader avoiding a punch in the face?

A Peking duck

What do you call evaluating someone by looking at them curiously?

Peer review

What do you call a cheap aunt?

Penny-ante

What do you call someone who always has a cat or dog?

PerPETual

What do you call a vulgar version of a book or play?

PerVERSION

Where do animals go to make out?

The petting zoo

How do police describe the crime of asphyxiation in the bedroom?

A pillowcase

What is a dance move you have to dry off after performing?

PiroWET (pirouette)

What do you call the location of a polling place?

A plebiSITE (plebiscite)

Why did the planning committee members take off their clothes?

They wanted to flesh out a solution.

What do you call a skin rash at Harvard or Yale?

Poison Ivy

What are the worst kind of lips?

PoLIPS (polyps)

Why did the Buddhist monk go to a pond?

To ponder

What do you call a small church owned by a large church?

A HOLY owned subsidiary (wholly)

Where do police officers wash their hands?

In the preSINK (precinct)

What do you call looking in the mirror before make-up is applied?

Preface

Which large, flowing stream is preferred by swans?

The SWANee River

What do you call being nervous right now?

Present tense

Where do candidates go to learn how to win an election?

Primary school

What do you call the charges at a steakhouse?

Prime rate

What do you call a beautiful trail of flowers?

A primrose path

When is it essential for the minister to use proper elocution during the wedding ceremony?

When he PRONOUNCES the bride and groom husband and wife.

What do you call a skinny person from Jerusalem?

An IsraeLIGHT (Israelite)

After the war, why did the leader of country A give the leader of country B a ring?

Because he wanted to propose terms for peace.

When are bar-hopping patrons like babies?

When they are on a pub CRAWL.

Why did the man take flowers to the active volcano?

He wanted to flirt with disaster.

What is served for lunch in Paris during a thunderstorm?

Quiche LorRAIN (Lorraine)

What condiment has the most enjoyment?

Relish

What do you call bandaging a gaping wound?

Rent control

Why did the trousers need a psychologist?

Because they were repressed.

Why did the terminal patient go on a Club Med vacation?

As a last resort

What do you call a stolen steak?

A purLOIN

What do you call it when a teacher changes an "A" to a "B"?

RetroGRADE

What do you call someone who works right next to motors?

EngiNEAR (engineer)

What is the highest card in the deck?

The one on top.

What is the most sarcastic part of a plant?

Its WRYzome (rhizome)

Which state is known for its streets?

ROAD Island (Rhode)

What's the best sport for someone who doesn't tell the truth?

Jai LIE (Alai)

What is an example of an edible road?

Sesame Street

What do you call a smart person who studies highways?

A ROAD Scholar (Rhode)

What do you call a beat-up meal in London?

Battered fish and chips

What do you call a nameless deer?

Jane Doe

What phrase describes a horse who has recovered from an illness?

In stable condition

Part 8

Why did the dishwasher stop his car?

Because there was a fork in the road.

Why did the optometrist go to Venice?

He wanted to examine EYEtalians (Italians).

What bird sings the saddest tune?

A swan's song

What is Chef Anthony's favorite pasta?

RigaTONY (rigatoni)

In which part of a play
does the big fight occur?

In the riot act

What do you call an old man
with well-defined muscles?

RIPPED van Winkle (Rip)

What is the most appropriate first name for a thief?

Rob

What do you call a pig with a driver's license?

A road hog

What bird could have won an Olympic medal?

Robin Hood

What do you call accommodations with neither television nor WiFi?

Room and bored

Why did the security guard walk in circles?

Because he was making the rounds.

What do you call dissatisfaction
with a massage?

Being rubbed the wrong way

What is the smartest flying insect?

A spelling bee

Why did the convict take
grammar courses in prison?

He wanted to
finish his sentence.

What do you call it when
there are animals in your sweat lodge?

Fauna in the sauna

How did 007 invest his money?

He bought a savings' BOND.

How do fish weigh things?

With their scales

What member of the sheep family always takes the blame?

The scapeGOAT

What do you call wireless internet access for Trekkies?

Sci-fi

Why did the reporter carry a small shovel?

He wanted to scoop the competition.

What's another name for test tube pregnancy?

AutoMATED

What do you call a golfer with an itch?

A scratch golfer

What do you call the driver of a van transporting prison guards?

A screwdriver

What do you call dressmaker anxiety?

SeamSTRESS

What do you call a violin that plays a note per second?

A second fiddle

What do you call being discharged from the Army due to gluttony?

Section ATE (eight)

Why did the self-deprecating man wear iron boots?

Because he was always shooting himself in the foot.

What do you call an assassin's art museum?

A shooting gallery

What do you call the midpoint between the two ends of a mall?

The shopping center

What kind of radio do surfers use?

Shortwave

How come the dealer couldn't find the casino?

He got lost in the shuffle.

What did the chef say when he had a hard time opening an oyster shell?

"Shucks"

What do you call color patterns on a hog?

PIGmentation

Where do attorneys confer after court?

At the sidebar

What do you call a karate strike to the body of your best friend?

A sidekick

What is the best medicine for eye pain?

A sight for sore eyes

What is the cleanest part of a football stadium?

The bleachers.

What is a Sillynym for Mr. Steak?

Sirloin

Why was Santa arrested?

For SLEIGHING (slaying)

Why did the soldier put on woman's clothes?

Because he wanted to skirt disaster.

What do you call a bribe paid to a plastic surgeon?

Skin graft

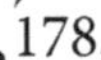

What do you call a tuber of trivial importance?

A small potato

What do you call a woman
who helicopters her children?

A SMOTHER

What mode of public transportation
is driven by an angel?

A nimBUS

What do you call
stealthy spies wearing
tennis shoes?

Sneakers

What is the cleanest
platform from which to speak?

A Soapbox

What was King Solomon's favorite animal?

Solomon's Seal

What is the most spiritual fish?

A holy mackerel

Why did the witch take remedial English classes?

She wanted to improve her spelling.

How did the police informant avoid having gas?

He spilled the beans.

What do you call a musical award ceremony for the AARP?

The grannies

What kind of fish loves to play with Barbies?
A DOLLphin
(dolphin)

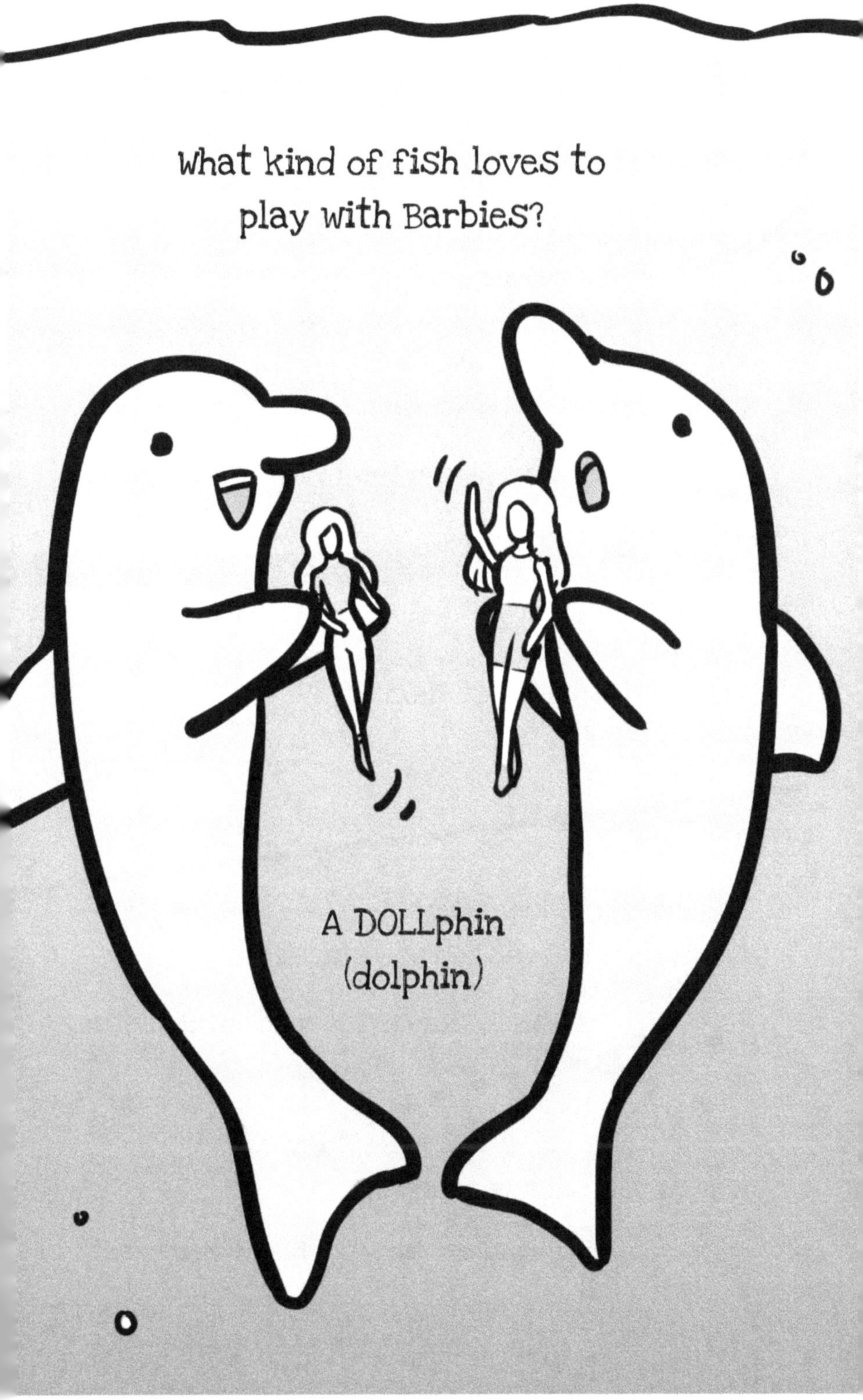

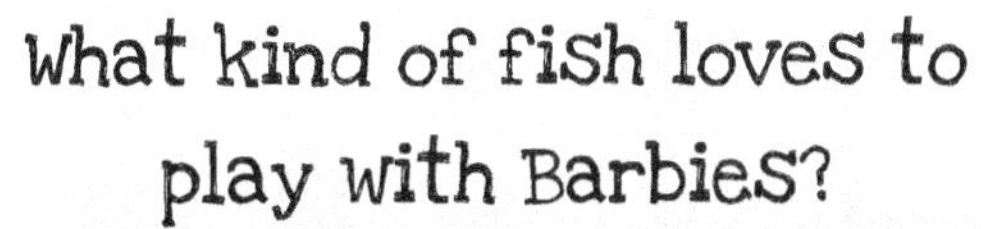

Why did the Tour de France racer listen to his wheels?

Because they spoke to him.

Why did the news reporter bring a butter knife to work?

Because he wanted to spread the news.

What bird is the most flexible?

A spread eagle

Why did the jockey kick his horse even before the race started?

It was a spur-of-the-moment decision

How do you kill a vegetarian?

Drive a steak through his or her heart.

Why did the criminal always drive cars with automatic transmission?

Because he was shiftless

Why did boy take shoe polish when he took his girlfriend out?

He took a shine to her

What powder speaks?

TALK powder (talc)

What do you call a challenge made in an appliance store?

A FRIGID DARE (Frigidaire)

What order of priests works with animals?

JeZOOit (Jesuit)

What kind of deer drinks wine?

BorDOE (Bordeaux)

What is the most precarious punctuation mark?

The asteRISK

What do you call being scared of ions?

IonoSFEAR (ionosphere)

What is the smartest dinosaur in the Language Arts?

The thesaurus

Where do you find the smartest combat soldiers?

In a think tank

What is the temperature of torture?

Third degree

What is something that can be changed but never exchanged?

The mind

What do you call potato chip crumbs?

Microchips

What is the angriest part of the day to have a meeting?

In the meantime

When do horses like to go to the movies?

They like to go to matiNEIGHS (matinees).

What do you call a dog with arthritis?

MaSTIFF

What do you call extreme sacrifice
for an inane reason?

MartyrDUMB (martyrdom)

Which kind of cereal crop causes headaches?

Migraine (grain)

What do you call a rodent marathon?

A rat race

What do you call a
commonsensible sum
in mathematics?

A rational number

What's a fancy term for stealing half of someone's food at dinner?

Reapportionment

Why did the Mother Superior always wear the same robe?

It was her habit.

What is the best remedy for a hangover?

A bungee cord

Where did the pregnant woman go to catch a train?

To the gesSTATION (gestation)

Why was the investor so interested in his family tree?

Because he was focused on the generation of income.

Why did the teacher give presents to her class?

Because she wanted them to be gifted students.

Why did the insecure girl buy eyeglasses?

Because she wanted to be good-looking.

What do you call an egg that never wins?

A goose egg

What color do you have to pay for?

Greens fee

What do you call the
night before a day of mourning?

GrEVE (grieve)

What is the best way to be in a rut?

To be groovy.

What prevented the Las Vegas showgirl from playing guitar?

She broke her G-string.

What do you call a horrible thing that becomes bigger?

GREW SOME (gruesome)

What do you call evidence that someone started a fire?

Flameproof

What is the ideal size for overweight people?

ExerSIZE (exercise)

What is the most important tense?

Existence

What do you call the measurement of mucus expelled by a cough?

ExpectoRATE

What do you call striking someone with a stare?

An eyelash

What does a conductor look at when the orchestra plays poorly?

He or she has to face the music.

What do you call a girl with too many suitors?

InunDATED

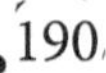

Part 9

Why does the IT manager always put five sheets of Bounce in every dryer load?
Because he likes SOFTWEAR (software).

Why were the yoga instructor's remarks viewed with skepticism?

Because to believe them was a stretch.

What do you call an automobile accident caused by a poorly maintained road?

ASFAULT (asphalt)

Why did the terminal patient go on a Club Med vacation?

As a last resort

What do you call a student loan at a military academy?

A caDEBT (cadet)

Why was the ox put on the ship?

To steer

What do you call it when a poet is not allowed into a bar or restaurant?

BARED (bard)

How does a cobbler make his shoe repair customers happy?

He conSOLES them.

What do you call an expert at waste disposal?

A connoSEWER (connoisseur)

What empire made the best living room furniture?

The Ottoman

What do you call flirting with other drivers on the freeway?

Traffic court

What is the unhappiest piece of equestrian gear?

The SADdle

What do you call a hypothesis after a hypothesis?

A second guess

Why did the girls like to watch the handsome chef trim and skin fruits and vegetables?

Because he had sex apPEEL (appeal).

Why do ghosts love bars?

Because of the BOOS (boose)

What is the price of an armed conflict called?

WarFARE

What is the favorite sport among male opera singers?

BASSball (baseball)

What flower says "hello" in Spanish?

A gladiHOLA (gladiola)

What is the slyest kind of sweater?

ArGUILE (argyle)

What did the sales clerk say to the customer who left the store after purchasing a sale item?

"Good-BUY" (bye)

Where do harsh, severe sailors sleep?

In the stern

What do you call a sorceress's knife?

A sWITCHblade

What branch of medicine should interior decoraters study?

ROOMatology (Rheumatology)

What do you call the French part of the foot?

ChaTOE (chateau)

What composer didn't lose?

GershWIN

Where is smell manufactured?

In the olFACTORY

What do you call someone who sits in for the horn player?

A substiTOOT (substitute)

What do you call a dog that barks at the lowest acoustic frequencies?

SubWOOFer

What do you call the repair of the end of a word?

SufFIX

Why did the salmon end the relationship with the shrimp?

Because the shrimp was SHELLFISH (selfish).

Where do swans go to get drunk?

To a swan dive

What holds up a pirate's pants?

The Swashbuckle

Why did the student bring a towel during the last week of school?

Because he was sweating through the final exams.

What do you call it when a Christmas tree has perfect form?

SymmeTREE (Symmetry)

What do you call an angry intersection?

A crossroad

What do you call immoral sentence structure?

SINtax (Syntax)

What do you call being quiet while sitting in a chair?

TaSIT (tacit)

What do you call the basic principle of thinking amusing thoughts?

FUNdaMENTAL

What charge is levied on a finger?

Thumb tax

What is a tight potato dish?

Tater TAUT (tot)

What structure saves you money?

Tax Shelter

Who is the cat's meow in class?

The teacher's pet

What do you call a Western Union message sent to your grandmother?

A teleGRAM

What famous archer must have been a raconteur?

William Tell

What do you call a teenager who smokes cigarettes?

NicoTEEN (nicotine)

What is the most defensible number?

TENable

What do you call it when racing dogs take a break?

A PAWS in the action (pause)

What do you call the destruction of a fence?

Defense

What do you call a restroom inside a tent?

Tepee

Where do sick passengers die?

In the terminal

In golf, what is a sillynym for mulligan?

A test-drive

What bird is synonymous with fungus?

Thrush

Why was the chef so impatient?

Because she was running out of THYME (time).

Why was the watchmaker consulted regarding a neurological patient's treatment?

To see what made the patient TICK (tic).

What do you call a premature parrot?

An early bird

Why did the candidate hire an oceanographer?

To determine the tide of public opinion

What is the best swimmer in the cat family?

Tiger Shark

What do you call the musical tone of wood?

TIMBER (timbre)

Where do they make Christmas tree decorations?

In Tinseltown

Why did the detective work undercover at a restaurant?

He needed a tip.

What is the worst thoroughfare for your lungs?

Tobacco Road

What do you call someone dedicated to being a baseball catcher?

ComMITted

Who were the original nerds from Mexico?

The TolTECHS (Toltecs)

What cookie requires you to pay a fee?

A Toll House Cookie

What is the most appropriate surname for an Irish handyman?

O'Toole

What do you call the choice of which dentures to buy?

A toothpick

Which food is the boss of all other food?

The top banana

Why wouldn't the actress reveal which blouse she was going to wear to the party?

It was TOP secret

What do you call a musical group with stolen instruments?

ContraBAND

What do you call a breach of contract suit regarding a cake?

A torte tort

Why was the lunar module given six points?

Because it made a touchdown.

Which
English
king was
a peeping
Tom?
King Leer
(Lear)

What do you call a lamp that curtsies?

PoLIGHT (polite)

What do you call delivering mink coats from point A to point B?

TransFUR (transfer)

What do you call a man who wears a dress that is too small?

A transvesTIGHT (transvestite)

Why did the director bring plastic bags to the premiere?

In case the critics trashed the movie.

What is the best currency to use in Prague?

Traveler's CZECHS (checks)

What do you call a male chef with a high voice?

Treble CHEF (clef)

What do you call applying primer to a ditch?

Trench coat

What do you call an angst-ridden vacation?

A guilt trip

What fish does best on interstate highways?

The turnPIKE

What bird is a part reptile?

A TURTLEdove

What do you call a ballerina on a train?

A tutu on a choo choo

Why was the girl friend in double trouble?

For two-timing her boy friend

What is the richest mammal?

TyCOON

How does a shadow cross a river?

It takes umBRIDGE (umbrage)

Who cooks the most savory food at home?

UMOMMY (umami)

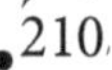

What do you call the mark underwear leaves on the skin?

Underline

What's a sillynym for "odd number?"

Uneven

What do you call a group of heart, liver and kidney donors?

An ORGANization

What do you call an all-female space mission?

An unmanned flight

What do you call a virtuous author?

WRITEeous (righteous)

What beard holds back water?

A Van DYKE (Dike)

What do you call being excluded from a group on account of physical stature?

OstraSIZED (ostracized)

What do you call the male offspring of a deer?

VeniSON

How do mallards cross rapid rivers?

They use the viaDUCK (viaduct).

What do you call an extremely nasty glass tube?

VILE (vial)

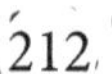

What do you call carpenters that work in law enforcement?

The VISE Squad (vice)

What do you use to communicate with a taxicab driver?

VoCABulary

What do you call the home of a serious bird?

EarNEST

Why was the mayor called IHOP?

Because he waffled on the issues.

What is the quietest plant at a party?

The wallflower

What is a celebration you want to stay away from?

A war party

What do you call a playful lion?

Big game

What kind of dog can tell you what time it is?

A watchdog

What do you call a bathroom debacle?

A waterloo

What insects have subtle differences?

NuANTS (nuance)

How did the protein congratulate the milk curd?

"Whey to go." ("Way")

What do you call a woman who has been married eight times?

Well-groomed

What was the policeman's status after he threw down his baton?

He was out of whack.

Why did the entrepreneur give sales' pitches on a bicycle?

Because he was wheeling and dealing.

What do you call a genius going to the restroom?

Whiz kid

What do you call it when a pig is determined?

Going whole hog

Why do laundry departments look for indecisive and ineffectual employees?

Because they are wishy-washy.

What kind of vehicles do witches drive?

Witchcraft

Why did the Chinese chef get into trouble?

He took a wok on the wild side.

What do you call the petition for an obese person's release from jail?

Writ of Habeas CORPULENT (corpus)

Why did the man give his fiancé a wet sponge?

Because he wanted her to have an engagement WRING (ring).

Why did the department store hire a hip-hop singer during Christmas?

For gift RAPPING (wrapping)

What do you call scribbles in George Washington's diary?

Yankee-Doodles

Why do knitters make great novelists?

Because they have so many yarns.

What do you call beer in Israel?

HeBREW

What do you call an alligator that interviews someone?

An interroGATOR

What do you call stopping places for angry people?

Stations of the cross

What is the most pugnacious state?

The state of war

What kind of luggage does an elephant take on a cruise?

A steamer trunk

What's a sillynym for tea inflation?

Steep prices

Part 10

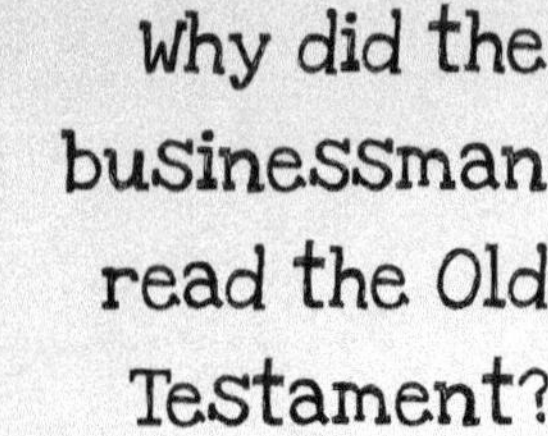

Because he was interested in PROPHETS (profits).

What do you call the surf report for Christmas day?

Yuletide

What do you call the union of two goats?

A zyGOAT (zygote)

Where do computer icons go for a drink?

The toolbar

What U.S. government official vacuumed crime?

J. Edgar Hoover

Who would have made a great wife for Noah?

Joan of ARK (Arc)

What do you call a person who makes phone calls impersonating someone else?

Phony

What diplomat had fantastic lips?

Kissinger

What city is known for its fireworks?

BANGkok

Why can't youth be re-captured?

Because it was never prisoner.

What is the deadliest kind of artillery used in a Holy War?

CANNONS of scriptures (canons)

How come they don't make them like they used to?

Because, being deceased, they don't make anything anymore.

What body part is in the import and export business?

The lungs

What celestial bodies do babies come from?

Honeymoons

What is the harm in taking everything with a grain of salt?

Hardening of the arteries

What silent sound can the deaf feel?

The sound of a rhyme

What is the most painful beverage?

A sucker punch

What do you call a metallic enemy?

An aluminum foil

What is the litigation attorney's favorite country-western song?

"A Boy Named Sue"

What is the most important personality trait to have in order to be a successful funeral home employee?

DEADication (dedication)

What do you call a frazzled bartender?

Stir-crazy

What do you call digging a ditch wearing a tuxedo?
DIGnity

www.ingramcontent.com/pod-product-compliance
Lightning Source LLC
Chambersburg PA
CBHW051759050726
47598CB00006B/2348

* 9 7 8 1 6 6 2 9 0 6 7 2 5 *